Boeing X-36

Tailless Agility Flight Research Aircraft

I0154910

Hugh Harkins

Boeing X-36 Tailless Agility Flight Research Aircraft

The publishers would like to thank the following for their assistance and contributions in the preparation of this publication: NASA Ames Research Centre; NASA Dryden Flight Research Centre; The Boeing Company and Lockheed Martin.

A Centurion Book

Published by Centurion Publishing
PO BOX 3268
Glasgow
G65 9YE

ISBN: 978-1-903630-19-8

First published 2013

Cover design © Centurion Publishing and Createspace

Page layout, concept and design © Centurion Publishing

Boeing X-36 *Tailless Agility Flight Research Aircraft*

The No.1 X-36 air vehicle flies over the Mojave Desert in southern California. NASA

"When you saw this aeroplane lift off, you saw the shape of aeroplanes to come," said Rod Bailey, X-36 program manager at NASA Ames Research Centre. The date was 17 May 1997; the place Dryden Flight Research Centre (DFRC), California, the event was the first flight of the remotely piloted X-36 tailless fighter technology demonstrator aircraft.

Tailless aircraft flight, however, was not a new concept. Since the 1930's and 1940's a number of tailless aircraft have made it into flight status and even into production in the case of the Northrop Grumman B-2A 'Spirit' 'Stealth bomber.' In the United States, Northrop in particular was heavily involved in tailless research and flying wing designs. When the Northrop N-1M made its first flight at Baker Lake, near Muroc, California on 3 July 1940,

it was claimed as the first true all wing powered aircraft in the world. Although lacking a vertical tail the N-1M had not completely relinquished all vertical control surfaces, having rudder surfaces in the down-turned wingtips, the angle of which could be varied from flight to flight. What appeared to be a large ventral fin was actually a faired tail-wheel designed to prevent auto-rotation on take-off. The Northrop N-1M was the forebear of the Northrop flying wing bombers, the XB-35, YB/YRB-49 and the B-2A of today.

Across the Atlantic, German designers were working on designs for a tailless flying wing jet fighter. The Horten brothers had flown a series of flying wing gliders beginning with the Horten I in 1931. In 1942, their work had reached the study phase for an operational flying wing jet fighter. The Horten IX V1 was a glider variant of the fighter prototype, later modified to fly with two BMW 003A turbojets, becoming the Horten V2.

Top and above: Northrop drew on its tailless experimental and development aircraft built in the 1930 and 40's to develop the XB-35 flying wing bomber. This design lost out to the Convair B-36 Peacemaker for a USAF production contract, but led to the jet powered YB-49, which also failed to enter service with the USAF. Northrop had to wait four decades for a tailless bomber design to enter service with the USAF in the shape of the B-2A Spirit. Both Northrop Grumman

Above: The Northrop Grumman B-2A 'Spirit' strategic bomber in service with the USAF is a tailless flying wing, designed as a 'stealth' penetrator requiring less support than its predecessors to penetrate heavily defended airspace. Its 'stealth' capabilities come mainly from the incorporation of low observable materials in its construction, but the tailless design also contributes to its unrivalled 'stealth' capabilities. USAF Below: The German Horten flying wing design.

Gliding trials commenced about May 1944 and the first powered flights began in January 1945. With the end of the war in Europe the program was buried under the rubble of Germany.

There were many other paper and flying tailless aircraft designs throughout the following decades including the Armstrong Whitworth AW.52 from Great Britain. This design flew in prototype form, but did not lead to a production variant.

As recently as 1990, the USN was planning for the McDonnell Douglas (MDC)/General Dynamics A-12 Avenger II strike aircraft. A high profile program, the A-12, developed under the ATA (Advanced Tactical Aircraft) program, was plagued by political and technical problems and was ultimately cancelled in January 1991. The program, which had been revealed in 1985 as a stealthy' subsonic all-weather deep penetration strike aircraft, was designed as an extremely 'stealth' driven flying wing. It would have been a two-seat strike aircraft capable of carrying a large payload in an internal weapons bay, with a combat radius of 1850-km (1,000-nm) without in-flight refuelling. A pair of up-rated non-afterburning derivatives of the General Electric F404 turbofan, which powered the MDC F/A-18 Hornet, would have powered it. This engine was originally known as the

Above: The Northrop YF-23 was developed for the USAF ATF competition, but lost out to the Lockheed YF-22. The YF-23, adopted a semi-tailless design with upward canted tail-planes doubling as the horizontal tails. USAF Below: An artist impression of the stillborn USN ATA.

F404/F5D2, but later matured into the F412-GE-400. To keep development costs down the A-12 had no realistic STOL (Short Take-Off and Landing) capability.

The first A-12 prototype Bu.No.164519 was initially expected to make its maiden flight in 1990, and some eight aircraft were to have been completed by the end of the year.

Following the revelation of program delays the first flight was grudgingly re-scheduled for mid-1991, and then again for March 1992. USN sources claimed that the contractors were experiencing difficulty in building the all-composite A-12 to the required specification weights which set out a loaded weight of 60,000-lb, slightly more than the Grumman A-6E which it was to replace. With the program facing increasing technical delays and cost increases it was cancelled in January 1991.

The A-12 Avenger II was not, however, designed for the extremely high agility levels which were to be explored by the X-36, which was designed for agile tailless flight, intended to revolutionise future fighter aircraft design. That said, it was designed as a tactical strike aircraft and would, therefore, bestow a degree of safe subsonic agility. With the addition of a thrust-vectoring system the A-12's high-alpha capability would have been improved, although the requirement for this would have been questionable.

8

Below right and bottom right: As with the YF-23, Northrop opted to forego conventional vertical tail-planes on its JSF contender. Following a number of design evolutions the horizontal stabilators were upturned at an angle of 25°, which differed considerably from the 40° elevation on the YF-23 (top). JSFPO and USAF

During the early phases of the USAF ATF (Advanced Tactical Fighter) competition some contractors including Rockwell put forward tailless proposals. The Northrop/McDonnell Douglas YF-23, while not dispensing with the vertical tail altogether, adopted a semi-tailless design with upward canted tail-planes doubling as the horizontal tail.

The YF-23, which was unofficially known as the 'Black Widow II', was designed and built as part of the Demonstration and Validation phase of the ATF program. The prototypes were 67.4-ft in length with a wingspan of 43.6-ft. The forward fuselage chines, which were reminiscent of those seen on the Lockheed SR-71 Blackbird, were carried over to the X-36. The large widely spaced tail surfaces were canted outward (or upward depending on your viewpoint) at 40°. However, this design lost out in the Demonstration Validation phase to the Lockheed/Boeing YF-22, which was developed into the F-22A Raptor, which entered initial operational service with the USAF on 15 December 2005.

The first YF-23, PAV-1 (Prototype Air Vehicle-1) conducted its maiden flight on 27 August 1990, followed by PAV-2 on 27 October that year. The two YF-23's flew more than 65-hours during the course of 50 flights, which included PAV-1 achieving 'super-cruise' (sustained supersonic flight without the use of afterburner) on its fifth flight. During the Demonstration Validation flight tests the YF-23 achieved a maximum speed of Mach 1.8, an Angle of Attack of 25°, manoeuvred at up to 7-g and super-cruised at Mach 1.43.

With the selection of the YF-22 as the USAF next generation fighter in April 1991, the YF-23's were grounded and both prototypes were transferred from Northrop to the NASA DFRC (Dryden Flight Research Centre) in 1993. There were no engines in the two aircraft and NASA had no plans to fly them in any research program, but had planned to use one of the two aircraft to study strain gage load calibration techniques, while the other would remain in storage at Dryden. However, both aircraft remained in storage until the summer of 1996, when the aircraft were transferred to museums.

The X-36 was officially unveiled on 19 March 1996, at McDonnell Douglas's St Louis plant in Missouri. Boeing

As with the YF-23, McDonnell Douglas and Northrop Grumman in partnership with British Aerospace opted to forego conventional vertical tail-planes on their losing JSF (Joint Strike Fighter) contender. Instead, the horizontal stabilators were upturned at an angle of 25°. This differed considerably from the 40-degrees elevation of the horizontal stabilators on the YF-23. Split ailerons on the wing trailing edge were used as rudders and airbrakes. Pitch and yaw control would have been provided by thrust vectoring, however, the team claimed that the aircraft would have been controllable throughout the entire flight envelope on aerodynamic controls alone.

While the MDC/NG/BAe (McDonnell Douglas/Northrop Grumman/British Aerospace) JSF design offered obvious advantages in terms of weight savings, reduced drag, and increased stealth effectiveness the design was rejected in favour of the more conventional Boeing and Lockheed Martin designs, which were selected to go on to the Concept Demonstrator phase of the JSF program. The Boeing aircraft received the designation X-32, while the Lockheed Martin design was allocated the X-35 designation. MDC was absorbed by Boeing in 1997 and Northrop Grumman and BAe (now BAE Systems) joined the Lockheed Martin JSF team.

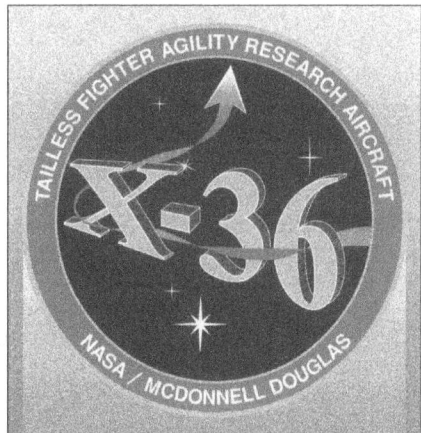

From the outset the X-36 was a joint NASA/McDonnell Douglas research effort aimed at demonstrating agile flight in a tailless fighter type aircraft design. Boeing

The futuristic lines of the X-36 are clearly evident in this view of an X-36 model from head-on and above. This type of early photograph release avoided showing the classified thrust-vectoring system, which was at the centre of the X-36's unique capabilities. Boeing

More recently a number of fourth generation fighter aircraft programs such as the Swedish Saab JAS 39 Gripen, the four-nation Eurofighter Typhoon and the French Dassault Rafale have involved studies of future quasi-tailless or tailless variants of their respective designs. Older generation aircraft like the Boeing F-15 Eagle have also been proposed in quasi-tailless and tailless variants. These are unlikely to move beyond the study phase. However, a Boeing F-15B designated the F-15 ACTIVE (Active Control Technology for Integrated Vehicles) has contributed to the development of tailless flight technology at the NASA Dryden Flight Research Centre.

Top and above: Two views of the X-36 model revealed in 1996. Both Boeing

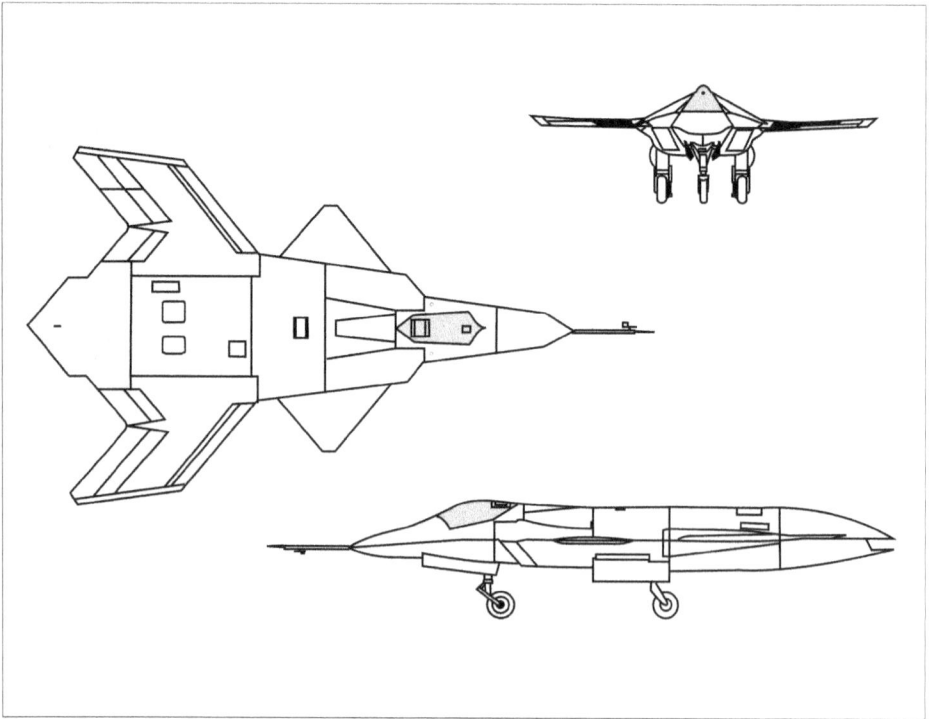

This 3-view general arrangement drawing (above) and line art (right) of the sub-scale X-36 clearly shows the unconventional lines of the X-36 design, including the complete absence of any vertical tail surface, which was a complete departure from current and past generation fighter aircraft design. Both NASA

The Indian MCA (Medium Combat Aircraft), which, appears to be an outgrowth of the Aeronautic Development Agency's Light Combat Aircraft (LCA), with no vertical tail surface was looked at in the early 2000's. The UK's FOAS (Future Offensive Air System) and the USAF's future strike platform will possibly incorporate tailless aircraft designs with artist impressions and concept drawings being released. These platforms may also emerge as UCAV (Uninhabited Combat Air Vehicles), an area which the US in particular is spending money to develop the necessary technologies that could enhance the safe and efficient use of UCAV's operationally,

resulting in the J-UCAS (Joint-Uninhabited Combat Air System) and its successors.

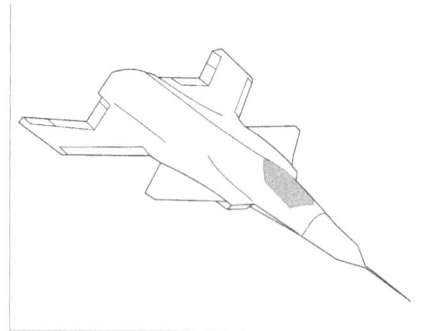

Other research platforms have been used to develop the technology that could bring the operation of tailless agile aircraft nearer to reality. In 1994/95, the Rockwell/MBB X-31 carried out a number of flights with software installed to demonstrate the feasibility of stabilising a tailless aircraft at supersonic speed using thrust vector control. The X-31's more recent VECTOR (Vectoring Extremely short take-off and landing Control and

14

Above and below right: Ground crew unpack the first X-36 vehicle from its packing crate following its arrival at the DFRC on 2 July 1996. Both NASA

Tailless operation Research) program also contributed to tailless flight technology research.

While thrust-vectoring control offers great potential for tailless agile flight other developing technologies are proving to be equally promising. Begun in 1996, the NASA AAW (Active Aero-elastic Wing) program later flight-tested an F-18 Hornet equipped with a modified wing, which could be twisted by aerodynamic forces to provide improved roll response at transonic and supersonic speeds for tactical aircraft.

The AAW program goal was to demonstrate aircraft roll control through aerodynamically induced wing twist on a full-scale high performance aircraft. This involved developing and transitioning the application of aero-elastic tailoring-based active flexible wing concepts through which traditional aircraft control surfaces such as ailerons and leading-edge flaps are used to twist a flexible wing. Roll manoeuvres are controlled by warping of the aircraft's wings.

On 19 March 1996, McDonnell Douglas Corporation and NASA (National Aeronautics and Space Administration) unveiled the newly declassified future fighter technology research aircraft designated X-36 at MDC's St Louis, Missouri headquarters. The X-36 program had its origins in a 1989 agreement between NASA AMC (Ames Research Centre) at Moffet Field, California and McDonnell Douglas, under which the latter had been contracted to develop technology breakthroughs, which would be required to achieve tailless agile flight. Based on the positive results of extensive wind-tunnel tests conducted in 1993, MDC proposed building a sub-scale tailless research aircraft to validate its wind-tunnel data with flight test results.

The No.1 X-36 vehicle sits on a hanger floor following its arrival at Dryden on 2 July 1996. NASA

In January 1994, MDC and NASA embarked on a joint program to build and test the remotely piloted tailless air vehicle with the aim of demonstrating the controllability of a highly agile tailless fighter aircraft design, the advantages of which would include reduced weight, drag and radar cross section.

There were many technological hurdles to overcome if the program was to be successful. MDC developed a flight control computer, which would overcome the aircraft's longitudinal and directional instability. NASA Dryden shared it's experience gained on the Highly Manoeuvrable Aircraft Technology (HiMAT) program, with NASA Ames, helping with the decision to avoid installing redundant flight control systems, which resulted in the X-36 cost being around one-fourth that of the HiMAT. This resulted in a higher

flight-test risk, but the risk problem was addressed by the installation of a simple, autonomous "fly-home" mode in the flight control computer, air data and inertial reference systems. This mode would automatically activate upon the loss of the controlling radio signal, sending the aircraft home for a safe landing. In the event that this failed the aircraft had an emergency parachute located in the top of the fuselage as a "last-chance" safety device.

The No.1 X-36 is carefully hoisted out of its packing crate at the Dryden Flight Research Centre on 2 July 1996. NASA

NASA DFRC shared with NASA Ames data on the HiMAT (Highly Manoeuvrable Aircraft Technology) research program conducted in the late 1970's and early 1980's. This resulted in the decision not to install redundant flight-control systems on the X-36, reducing program costs and aircraft weight and complexity. Producing a second X-36, which could replace the first in the event of loss or damage, partially offset the lack of redundancy. NASA

The two remotely piloted HiMAT aircraft were flown at Dryden from mid-1979 to January 1983. They were used to demonstrate advanced fighter aircraft technologies that could be used in the future development of high performance military aircraft. The HiMAT drones were air-launched from the Centre's venerable Boeing B-52 Mother ship. Unlike HiMAT, the X-36 was designed to take off under its own power.

Two X-36 flight vehicles were ordered and these were built at MDC St Louis facility. The construction of two aircraft ensured that the data that was

required from the X-36 flight-test program would be acquired in the event that one of the flight vehicles was lost. NASA was responsible for continued development of critical technologies while MDC was responsible for aircraft fabrication.

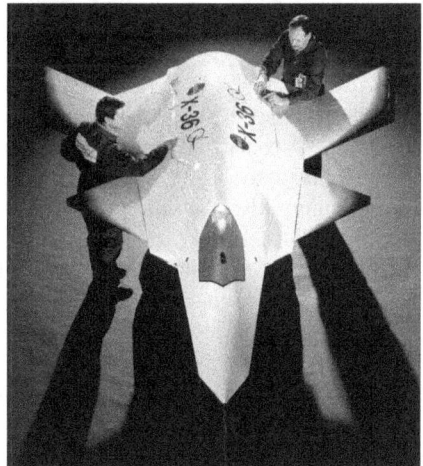

The scale of the X-36 is illustrated here, while engineers at McDonnell Douglas's Phantom Works at St Louis are working on the vehicle. Boeing

Above and right: The X-36 conducted a series of high-speed taxi tests on Rodgers Dry Lake Bed, Edwards AFB in October 1996, in preparation for the sub-scale vehicles flight-test program. Both NASA

Final assembly of the first X-36 demonstrator aircraft commenced in June 1995, some 17 months after MDC and NASA officially embarked on the $17m programme. This flight vehicle was constructed in just 28 months using rapid prototype methods pioneered at the McDonnell Douglas Phantom Works in St Louis. Among these techniques were: advanced software development tools for rapid avionics prototyping; low-cost tooling moulds; composite skins cured at low temperatures without the use of autoclaves and high speed machining of unitised assemblies. Off the shelf components were used whenever possible to keep the cost of the program down and speed up development.

The X-36 program was never intended to produce a prototype for a full-scale fighter aircraft, but rather to act as a flying technology demonstrator for future technologies, providing design options and tools for designers

of future fighter aircraft and or Uninhabited Combat Air Vehicles.

The X-36 demonstrator was the first fighter type aircraft designed from the outset without vertical or horizontal tails in the US. The aircraft shows the design heritage of the Northrop/MDC Corporation YF-23 losing Advanced Tactical Fighter contender and the unsuccessful McDonnell Douglas/Northrop Grumman/British Aerospace JSF design. The X-36 also exhibits basic low-observable design features such as aligned control surfaces which are also design heritage from the YF-23 and the above mentioned JSF team. MDC's X-36 Program Manager Dave Manley confirmed that the company entered the

On 6 November 1996, a USN Bell HH-1N
helicopter took the X-36 aloft for radio
frequency and telemetry tests. The tests
were conducted over Rodgers Dry Lake
Bed. NASA

project with NASA 'for two main
reasons.' "Firstly because there is a lot
more interest now in tailless vehicles
and secondly, and the reason we put up
$10m dollars of the $17m dollar X-36
program cost was because we wanted to
demonstrate the Phantom works
capability for rapid prototyping." Other
funding came from NASA's Office of
Aero-Space Technology. The X-36
program benefits included the hoped
for breakthrough in technology, such as
the vehicles 'advanced aerodynamics,
unique thrust-vectoring system and
advanced control laws that couple the
whole thing together.'

Above: The X-36 is placed firmly back on the ground as the Bell HH-1N hovers over the Dry Lake Bed following completion of the radio frequency and telemetry tests. Right: The X-36 hangs from its tether as ground crew prepare to secure the vehicle. Both NASA

The X-36 vehicles are basically a 28% scale remotely piloted fighter design. Reducing the scale to 28% allowed the aircraft to be powered by a single 3.1- kN (700-lb) thrust William's F112 turbojet engine, originally developed for the McDonnell Douglas (now Boeing) AGM-129 Advanced Cruise Missile (ACM). The availability of these power plants was partially responsible for the scaling of the vehicles. Some 80-kg (176-lb) of fuel is carried, enough for a flight duration of around 30-45 minutes. MDC figures credit the X-36 with a wingspan of 3.6-m (11-ft), a length of 6.3-m (19-ft), a height of 1-m and a weight of 495-kg (1,090-b) empty and 590-kg (1,298-b) at maximum take-off weight. MDC claimed that a potential speed of 350 to 400-kt (650-740 km/h) was possible,

but testing was to be limited to around a maximum of 160-180-kt to prevent the structure failing in the event of a worse case flight control system failure.

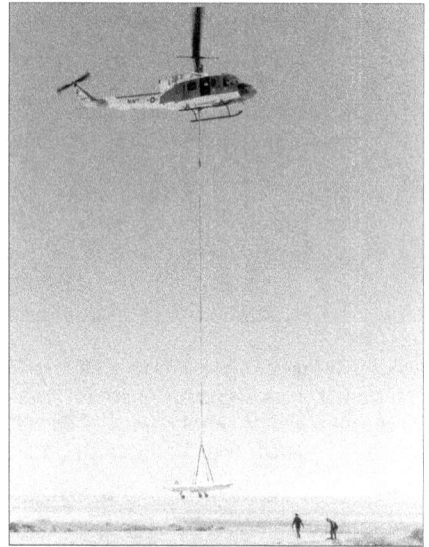

The airframe structure is made of machined aluminium, covered with largely composite skins. The fuselage is skinned with LTM-10 composite, which does not require curing in an

20

Above and below right: Under the early morning sunrise, engineers prepare the X-36 for its maiden flight on 17 May 1997. Both NASA

autoclave, while the wings are skinned with IM7 composite. LTM10 is also used to form the bifurcated inlet/diffuser sub assembly, which is scaled directly from the Boeing (formerly McDonnell Douglas) F/A-8E/F Super Hornet design. The intake lips of the inlet are blunted, having a larger radius to suit the slow speed-operating envelope of the X-36, which was flown at speeds up to 177-kt.

Control surfaces on the X-36 consist of all-moving canard fore-planes and split ailerons and flaperons on the aft set wing. Three ailerons are mounted on the trailing edge of the wing, which is sharply cranked towards mid-span increasing the aircraft's low observable characteristics. The two outboard sections function independently and split to provide yaw control (using drag) while the inner section acts like a 'typical flaperon', the ailerons raising and lowering asymmetrically for pitch and roll control. The aircraft's advanced single channel Honeywell developed Matrix-X digital auto-code Fly-By-Wire (FBW) Flight Control System (FCS) was developed with

commercially available components and was used in the McDonnell Douglas DC-XA 'Clipper Graham' and later adopted for the McDonnell Douglas (now Boeing) F-15 ACTIVE research program conducted at Dryden. The fly-by-wire flight control system integrates control inputs using the split ailerons and a thrust-vectoring control system providing yaw control to compensate for the absence of conventional tail surfaces.

The X-36 demonstrator's thrust-vector nozzle provides the initial control input until its limits are reached, at which point the split ailerons gradually take over. NASA X-36 Program Manager Larry Bricklebaw explained that the thrust-vectoring system was based on a design that was developed by McDonnell Douglas

Above and below right: Final pre-flight preparations are conducted on the No.1 X-36 vehicle prior to its first flight in the early morning of 17 May 1997. Both NASA

during the late 1980's. It is understood that the system deflects engine exhaust in the yaw axis only, probably through a set of vertically mounted veins with the gases exiting through a flattened exhaust nozzle which is recessed slightly beneath the aircraft's broad 'beaver' tail. When the X-36 was rolled-out in 1996, the thrust-vectoring system was deliberately hidden from view.

Although thrust-vectoring control is a key element of the X-36 design, because the X-36 was designed to be tailless from the beginning the design philosophy does not actually require thrust-vectoring to control the aircraft, therefore, it would still be flyable in the event of a thrust-vectoring nozzle "lockup" or other failure. According to the NASA Program Manager, the X-36 was designed to maintain level one handling capability and be controllable even when the engine power had been lost or the vectoring nozzle was locked

inadvertently in the one position. The design team were looking for yaw power without a tail and basically ended up with what the Northrop Grumman B-2 Spirit 'Stealth' bomber team did. The B-2 has a lot more span, so the X-36 team had a tougher job, instead of the flaps opening symmetrically the upper and lower surfaces separate or move together as an aileron.

The X-36 wing shape was driven by the sweep, fore-planes were added to increase pitch down control authority and move through +10° to -80° to compensate for the large pitch up movement generated by the chinned fore-body at high angles of attack. They needed to be large to help destabilise the aircraft.

Top and above: The X-36 got air under its wheels under its own power for the first time on 17 may 1997, when the aircraft climbed into the air over Rodgers Dry Lake Bed reaching an altitude of 4,900-ft during the flight, which lasted around five minutes. Both NASA

The X-36 is flown by a pilot controller in a virtual cockpit-complete with Heads-Up Display (HUD) in a ground station with a video camera mounted in the nose of the aircraft providing the ground station crew with a forward view from the aircraft. The man in-the-loop approach eliminated the need for an expensive and complex autonomous flight control system.

The lack of any vertical tail surfaces is shown in this side on view of the X-36 during its maiden flight. NASA

The designers of the X-36 Ground Control Station (GCS) cockpit resisted any temptation to reduce the cockpit control and display suite. As the pilot has less "natural cues of peripheral vision, sounds and kinesthetic feedback", the X-36 team had to provide replacements for these missing cues in order to create an "overall situational awareness comparable to a full-sized aircraft". The design team ruled out motion bases and buffet simulation cues and instead concentrated their efforts on audio, visual and HUD cues. The cockpit design benefited from technology salvaged from the cancelled A-12 Avenger II ATA. This included a full-sized stick, rudder pedals and their respective feel systems, throttle and a full complement of HOTAS (Hands On Throttle And Stick) switches complete the cockpit control effectors.

The GCS cockpit was equipped with two large 20-in display screens which provided visual displays to the ground-based pilot. In addition the information from the screens was "redundantly located throughout the GCS". The X-36

canopy mounted cockpit displayed down-linked video imagery which was shown as background on the forward viewing display screen

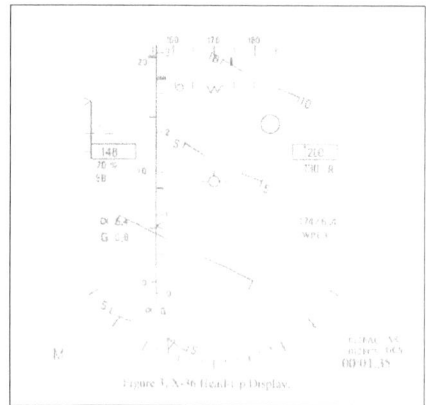

The ground based pilot controller views an onboard HUD (Heads-Up Display) image showing various flight data such as speed, altitude and heading. NASA

The GCS cockpit could also be used as a simulator, during which "a synthetic terrain data base showed the Edwards AFB vicinity including the main and lakebed runways." The heads-up display "overlays the video with embedded flight test features."

The X-36 over Edwards AFB during its 5th flight on 26 June 1997. NASA

The second cockpit display HSI, shows fuel and engine data as well as control surface deflections, yaw rate and a number of "warnings, cautions and advisories" for the pilot. An audio signal known as ("tweedle-dee") alerts the GCS to new warnings or cautions. In the event that either of the two display screens suffered a malfunction or even completely failed, an adjacent monitor that was shared by the X-36 test director and the GCS engineer served as a backup.

The X-36 ground cockpit HUD "was designed to overlay exactly the down-linked video and to have 1:1 registration with the outside world. Digital readouts of airspeed, altitude, AOA, and Nz are typical of the F/A-18 and F-15E HUDs. Navigational bearing and distance to the selected steer point shows in the NAV block; steering points are selectable by HOTAS."

As mentioned the GCS design included audio cues for the pilot. Jet and wind noise was included in the simulator in an attempt to make the flights more realistic for the operator and a microphone was installed in the aircraft cockpit area allowing the aircraft engine noise to be down-linked to the ground cockpit. The X-36 ground station pilot pointed out those audio cues alerted the team "more than once" to in-flight problems which, included engine stalls which were dealt with before they became serious, and screech at high power settings.

Top right: The X-36 lifts-off from Rodgers Dry Lake Bed. Above: The forward canards are deflected showing their large size in relation to the aircraft. Both NASA

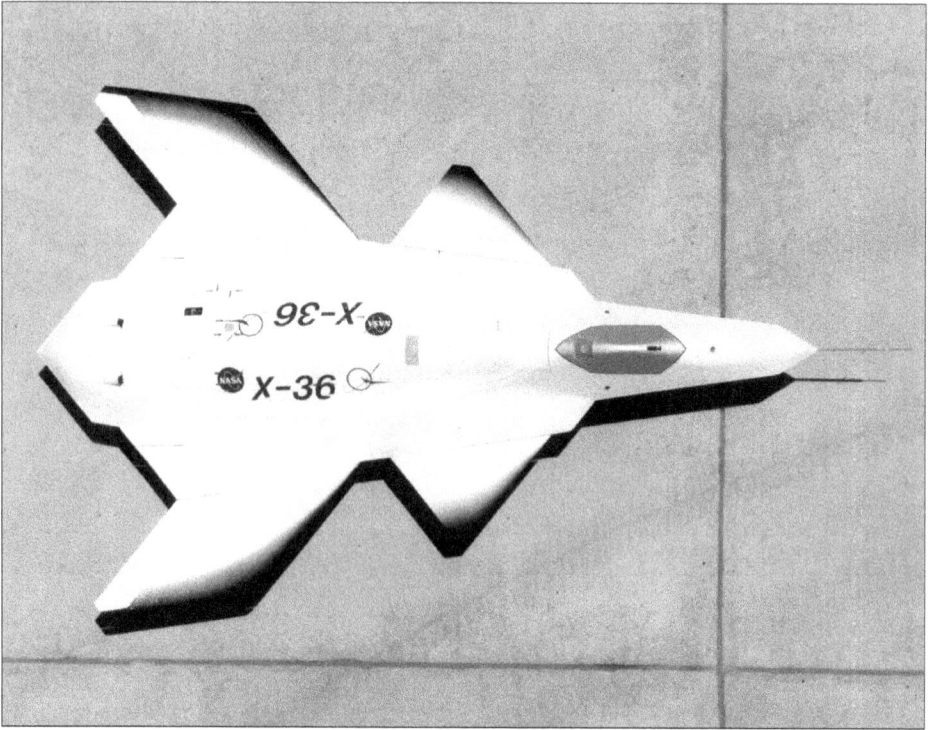

Top: As it was designed as a vehicle to demonstrate tailless agile flight only, the X-36 lacked any radar absorbent coatings, although the design incorporated shaping's, which would reduce radar signature of a full-scale aircraft in comparison to the then current operational fighter aircraft. Much of the X-36 design heritage would be incorporated into the later Boeing X-45 UCAV (Uninhabited Combat Air Vehicle) demonstrator. Above: In 2001, Boeing unveiled the 'Bird of Prey' technology demonstrator, which it had flown during 1996. This piloted aircraft demonstrated technologies applicable to future tailless combat aircraft design including UCAV's. The nose of the Bird of Prey bears a similarity to that adopted for the later X-45A. Boeing

The X-36 overflies the landscape of southern California in June 1997. The first few flights of the vehicle encountered problems, some of which required the flight-duration to be reduced or the flight terminated. NASA

When the X-36 program was revealed in March 1996, it was expected that the flight test program would begin in June that year, but it would be almost a year later before the first X-36 flight vehicle finally took to the air under its own power. The MDC/NASA team predicted that all the required flight test data for the initial flight test program would be collected over 25 sorties and the initial flight test program was expected to be completed in around six months. Much of the research was to focus on the aircraft's single channel propulsion and complex integrated flight control system.

The flight test program was conducted at NASA's Dryden Flight Research Centre, Edward's Air Force Base, California and the first X-36 arrived there on 2 July 1996. The aircraft arrived as freight and was removed from its packing crate and into

its hanger at the flight test centre. In the work up to the flight test program a series of ground testing commenced during the second half of 1996. High-speed taxi tests were conducted on Rogers Dry Lake Bed on 17 October 1996. During the taxi tests the aircraft was tested at speeds up to 85 knots. Normal take-off speed would be 110 knots at rotation. A few weeks later, on 6 November, an USN Bell HH-1N helicopter lifted the X-36 off the ground for radio frequency and telemetry tests above Rogers Dry Lake. The purpose of taking the X-36 aloft for the radio and telemetry systems checkouts was to test the systems more realistically while airborne. Further taxi and radio frequency tests were carried out along with other ground based testing as the X-36 vehicle was prepared for its first flight.

The No.1 X-36 made its first flight from Rodgers Dry Lake Bed on Saturday 17 May 1997, lifting off at 7:08 PDT (Pacific Daylight Time). A Saturday was chosen so as to avoid any disruption with the main air traffic at Edwards AFB on weekdays. At the

Photographs released of early flight-testing were taken at angles designed to carefully conceal the classified thrust-vectoring system. This later photograph of the aircraft flying over the Dry Lake Bed in October 1997 clearly shows the thrust-vectoring exhaust. NASA

request of the X-36 Team, the UAV (Uninhabited Air Vehicle) operating areas provided an additional operating area close to the data-link antenna.

The X-36 take-off was as had been simulated with the air vehicle lifting off at the predicted airspeed shown with the simulator. Climb angle was around 15 degrees; good even considering that the undercarriage gear and flaps remained down. About two minutes into the flight a temperature caution occurred. The data that was down-linked indicated that the nozzle bay temperatures were climbing, resulting in an immediate decision to terminate the flight. The ground based pilot controller noted, "I knew nearly immediately after takeoff that the airplane was flying well. Control responses appeared immediate and the damping appeared good. No obvious deficiencies were noted." The decision to abort the flight meant there was no time for any traditional test maneuvers as the team focused on repositioning the aircraft for an immediate landing, bringing the 6-mimute flight to an end. The ground-based pilot controller noted, "Since the air-mass velocity vector was our airborne default, I noticed the first problem now with it - it wasn't yet accurate enough to use as a glide slope reference. The theory was that if the velocity vector was placed about 1 degree down, then sink rate should be about $1/60^{th}$ of the true airspeed. However, this was not to be the case. Since I had never made a lakebed landing with a sight picture only 3-ft above the lakebed, I was cautious to avoid the sinkhole illusion and tried to fly the air-mass velocity vector to set sink rate. After about half the runway disappeared behind me, it appeared that I had virtually no sink rate and I reset the velocity vector about 2½ degrees low. This appeared to do the trick as the X-36 made an uneventful, but gentle touchdown and rollout."

Above: The X-36 is displayed on the ramp at Dryden along with, from clockwise left to right; the F-15 ACTIVE, SR-71, F-106, F-16XL#2 and X-38. This represented a portion of the Dryden fleet in July 1997. Right: The X-36 during a test-flight overt the Mojave Desert in June 1997. Both NASA

"In retrospect, the up-wash predictions were about 1½ degrees too low with the effect that the air-mass velocity vector showed about 1½ degrees lower than the actual flight path. Until the new up-wash data could be incorporated, we selected the inertial velocity vector for all remaining landings." Following the first flight the fault was rectified by MDC engineers by fitting two small air scoops to improve nozzle bay cooling.

During its reduced duration first flight the remotely piloted aircraft attained an altitude of 4,900-ft (1500-mt) and a speed of 147-kt (270-km/h). The first flight, despite its shortened duration and impromptu ending, demonstrated the aircraft's good stability and easy handling. Control surface activity was

minimal compared to conventional tailed FBW (Fly-By-Wire) aircraft.

The second flight of the X-36 was no less eventful than the first and according to the test team provided more significant problems. About 10 miles out from Edwards AFB, while flying at an altitude of 12,000-ft the signals from the on board video and the downlink "suddenly became very weak with the presence of static and video noise. A break X then appeared which meant that the X-36 had gone into lost link autonomous operation." The X-36 team immediately began implementing recovery procedures to try and re-establish the data link with the aircraft.

This view of the X-36 seen during Phase three flight-testing, which commenced on 30 October 1996, shows to advantage the extent of wing-body blending incorporated into the 'stealthy' design. NASA

As the ground based engineers attempted to regain communication with the aircraft, the independent NASA range safety display was used to track the X-36 vehicle. "In the autonomous mode, the aircraft turns to the nearest steering point and then navigates back on a preplanned return route to the autonomous orbit point located over the northern part of Rogers Lakebed. As bad luck would have it the nearest autonomous steering point was behind the aircraft, farther away from the station. A couple of times I regained control momentarily only to lose links in a matter of seconds. Each time the link was briefly regained, the aircraft was seen in a turn towards the more distant, but closer (to the aircraft) steering point. Each glimpse of the intermittent link showed a yet steeper angle of bank, well beyond what we had yet flown. Even so, the autonomous autopilot handled it well, although it was much more aggressive than we had seen in our simulation of this type of emergency. (Adjustment of its aggressiveness would also be high on our work list.) Fortunately, the X-36 returned to the autonomous orbit point where control was finally regained and an uneventful, but stress filled, landing was made. After the problem was finally corrected, we had no further data link problems."

There were also some problems on the third and fourth flights when data link failure resulted in a temporary loss of contact with the X-36, resulting

in the aircraft reverting to autopilot until ground control contact could be re-established.

The first phase of the flight program was completed on 30 June 1997, with the last four flights being conducted between 27 and 30 June. On completion of the first phase of flight testing NASA/MDC announced that the X-36 had achieved a higher angle of attack (AoA) than was planned during the aircraft's initial eight flights. The original plan was for a 15° AoA in phase 1, but as the flight controls worked so well and handling qualities and stability margins were better than predicted an AoA of 20° was achieved. The No.1 X-36 was put through a number manoeuvres and was flown to +2-g.

Of the PID (Parameter IDentification), used to determine individual control-surface effectiveness, and RTSM (Real Time Stability Margin), used to monitor flight control phase and gain margins, it was stated that the NASA-developed real-time stability-margin 'was a key element in successfully completing phase 1 in record time.'

'During Phase One flight testing, the X-36 team gathered a considerable amount of data. Real Time Stability Margin and Parameter IDentification maneuvers were flown with the aid of automated control sweeps, singlets and doublets, which were uplinked to the aircraft. When the pilot squeezed the trigger the maneuver started and was complete in a matter of seconds. Throughout, the pilot could still control the X-36, although the engineers preferred as little pilot input as possible. These automated maneuvers greatly facilitated envelope expansion.'

The X-36 program accumulated a wealth of data, which would be used in later programs including the X-45 UCAV, which paved the way for the J-UCAS (Joint Uninhabited Combat Air System) and later programs. NASA

Rolling maneuvers at three different speeds completed the testing of Phase 1. 'Handling qualities were remarkably good, but a bit of pitch wobble caused Cooper-Harper ratings of HQR-4 for the pitch attitude capture task. Bank angle capture was assessed at HQR-3. There was also an unusual spiral divergence, which tended to steepen all bank angles and required some lateral stick deflection towards wings-level for all turns. Considerable pilot attention was required. I was very glad that we had invested the extra effort to provide good situational awareness and minimize pilot distraction.' 'The last four flights of Phase 1 were flown in only four working days, attesting to the excellent reliability of the X-36.'

Phase 1 Flight Test - Thrust Vectoring on. (100–160 knots, 0 to 15 degrees AoA, Nz 0.2 to 3 g)

• Initial Handling Quality Assessment

• Functional Checkout

• Real-Time Stability Margin Assessment (RTSM)

• Air Data Calibration

• Parameter IDentification (PID)

• 360° Rolls

Achieved:

• Upper Level 2 Handling Qualities

• 2 g, 20° AoA, 160 KEAS

• 8 Flights, 4 Hours Flight Time

Following phase 1 testing the aircraft was grounded for upgrades to the NASA developed flight control software, which allowed improved stability margins at higher AoA. The new software enabled the stability margin to be determined in real time and Parameter Identification software developed by MDC enabled the aircraft to be utilised as a flying wind tunnel.

The second of the two X-36 vehicles was due to fly in June 1997, but was delayed, and the test team hoped to fly the aircraft in August, but the success

By the time Phase Three was complete, the X-36 had conducted 31 flights, with a total flight time of 15 hours and 38 minutes. NASA

of the first aircraft negated the need for the second aircraft and it remained firmly on the ground.

During phase 2 of the program, which began on 29 July 1997 and ended in September that year, the No.1 X-36 flight vehicle continued to perform exceptionally well. It proved to be more agile than the most manoeuvrable fighter aircraft in the world at the time. "After 22 test flights the aircraft continued to perform flawlessly" and according to Boeing (which had absorbed MDC) exceeded performance expectations. The manoeuvres it had performed up to this time went "far beyond the capabilities of the F/A-18 Hornet - the top standard for agility in fighter aircraft" (this latter statement

was inaccurate as many combat aircraft were in service with agility levels that far exceeded those of the F/A-18, even when it entered service in the early 1980's.) The 22nd flight was also the final flight of Phase 2 flight-testing.

During this phase the X-36 completed all planned low and high-g agility manoeuvres, demonstrating the aircraft's ability to quickly perform under a wide range of aerodynamic loads. These manoeuvres included 360° rolls at AoA (Angles of Attack) up to 15° and rapid turning rolling manoeuvres up to 35° AoA. By 24 September 1997, the X-36 had flown for 10 hours and 54 minutes, performed at maximums of 4.86-g, 40° AoA, 177-kt air speed and 20,500-ft altitude. During the Phase 1 and 2 testing, the team was able to fly the X-36 up to five days in a row; then claimed as an unprecedented feat in the flight testing of remotely piloted vehicles.

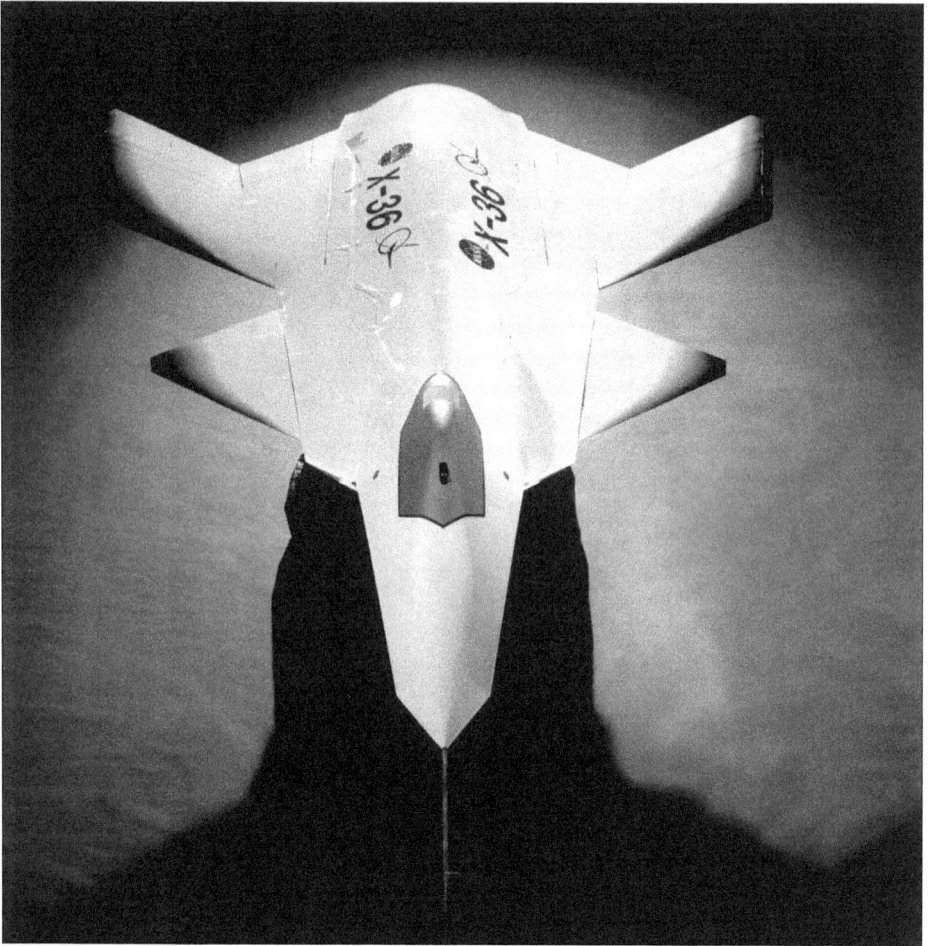

Once the initial X-36 test program was complete the aircraft was grounded before being briefly reinstated to flight test status in 1998 for the RESTORE program. Boeing

Phase 2 testing expanded the flight envelope. With the new control laws stability margins were improved and better derivatives were available. This resulted in still better flying qualities, increasing to Level 1 ratings in all axes. The Ground Station Pilot noted, "With the new improvements, accelerated g bank-to-bank rolls, or RPOs (rolling pullouts) were flown at mid range speeds at up to 4.8-g. Whether lateral stick was used, or rudder pedal, roll rates were spectacular and exceeded the program goals by a significant margin. These rates exceeded those of any aircraft I've flown by a dramatic margin. Reliability was also very good in this phase with 14 flights completed in only 35 calendar days. Seven of those were flown in only 8 working days."

Phase 2 Flight Test

(60–160 knots, 0 to 35° AoA, Nz 0.2 to 5-g)

Elevated g Agility ~120 knots

2A: Air Data Calibration, RTSM, PID

2B: Incorporate 2A Results

Agility Demo - Thrust Vectoring ON

Agility Demo - Thrust Vectoring OFF

Achieved:

Level 1 Handling Qualities

4.8-g, 40° AoA, 177 KEAS (177 kts)

22 Flights, 10.9 Hours Flight Time

Following the completion of Phase Two, the X-36 was again grounded for FCS (Flight Control System) upgrades incorporating the results of Phase 2 testing, prior to the beginning of Phase 3 flight testing, which commenced with the 23rd flight on 28 October 1997. Between then and 12 November that year, the X-36 conducted a further eight flights, completing the flight research phase of the program on that date with the last flight lasting 34 minutes.

During Phase Three, the X-36 demonstrated manoeuvres at lower speeds and high AoA. By the time the flight-testing was complete the X-36 had flown a total of 31 times for a total of 15 hours and 38 minutes flight time. The program met or exceeded all project goals with a maximum altitude of 20,500 ft being attained and a maximum angle of attack of 40°. The key to the program success was the Flight Control Software and a total of four different versions were used during the flight testing of the vehicle. The program had demonstrated the feasibility of future tailless fighter aircraft to achieve levels of agility far superior to the best fighter aircraft then in service or in development.

During the initial test program, only the first X-36 vehicle was flown and this aircraft was grounded when the program was wrapped up following the 12 November 1997 flight. However, the X-36 was given a new lease of life when it was decided that the aircraft could still be a valuable tool in other research programs. To this end NASA Ames Research Centre transferred control of the X-36 research aircraft to the NASA Dryden Flight Research Centre on 9 December 1998, for future flight tests.

The ARL (Air Force Research Laboratory) at Wright Patterson Air Force Base, Dayton Ohio utilised the X-36 vehicles for its RESTORE (Reconfigurable Systems for Tailless Fighter Aircraft) flight tests at Dryden. The RESTORE program used advanced flight control software to respond to a variety of battle damage and hardware failures. It demonstrated technology that increased aircraft survivability and significantly reduced life cycle costs of military and commercial aircraft.

Top: The X-36 program was of immense value to designers of next generation combat aircraft including UCAV's. NASA **Above: The X-36 as it is displayed in the USAF Museum.** USAFM

The RESTORE flight test program was a joint effort funded by the Air Force Research Laboratory, NASA Dryden Flight Research Centre, and the Naval Air Systems Command (NAVAIR), Patuxent River, Maryland. The Boeing Company retained ownership of the X-36 aircraft and its Phantom Works division developed the RESTORE technology that would be used in the research program.

The X-36 is formally inducted into the National Museum of the USAF at Wright Paterson AFB, Ohio, with the huge bulk of a Boeing B-52D Stratofortress strategic bomber in the background. Boeing

In December 1998, two RESTORE research flights were flown with the adaptive neural-net software running in conjunction with the original proven control laws, proving the viability of the software approach. Several in-flight simulated failures of control surfaces were introduced as a problem for the re-configurable control algorithm. Each time, the software correctly compensated for the failure and allowed the aircraft to be safely flown in spite of the degraded condition.

With the flight research program completed, the two X-36 aircraft were kept in flyable storage at Dryden in case they were adopted for other research programs.

The success of the original flight test program and the increasing interest in tailless flight is opening up new doors for technologies pioneered by the X-36 demonstrator which are applicable to future operational aircraft, particularly in the Uninhabited Combat Air Vehicle field, which is being developed by a number of nations during the first and into the second decade of the 21st Century The X-36 has shown the way forward for future combat aircraft design, particularly in the area of UCAV's.

The low key end to the X-36 program and the fact that the latest US tactical fighter program, the Lockheed Martin F-35 Lightning II (Joint Strike Fighter), has conventional vertical tails does not signal a waning of interest in tailless fighter designs. What does, however, seem likely is that the UCAV will be at the forefront of future tailless tactical aircraft design. These vehicles will in all probability remain subsonic, at least in the near term and will not require the levels of agility that inhabited fighters require for combat manoeuvring. That said UCAV will be required to be manoeuvrable enough to take evasive action and to avoid collisions in dense air traffic control airspace.

The Future Aircraft Technology Enhancement (FATE) program was launched with the aim of achieving quantum leaps in technology, which could be applied to future military and commercial aircraft. In the late 1990's it was speculated that the FATE program would receive the designation X-39. However, no designation was applied and the X-39 designation has not as yet been allocated.

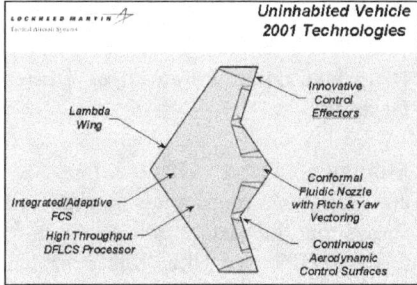

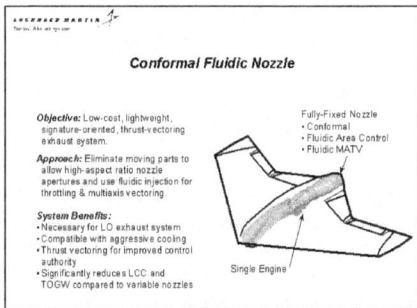

Top and above: These two diagrams are from a 1997 Lockheed Martin FATE report showing a vision of what was expected to be year 2001 UCAV technologies. Both Lockheed Martin

The following data comes from a 1997 FATE report:

"Examples of FATE technologies include affordable low-observable data systems, active aero-elastic wing, robust composite sandwich structures, advanced compact inlets, photonic vehicle management systems, self-adaptive flight controls and electric actuation.' Both Boeing and Lockheed performed a long-range study on next-generation aircraft.

A subset of the national Fixed Wing Vehicle (FWV) Program, FATE was structured with three phases:

- FATE I, Phase I: Define a set of aircraft technologies that must be flight test validated in a new air vehicle to meet FWV Phase I program goals for a fighter attack class of aircraft, including both inhabited and uninhabited aircraft.

- FATE I, Phase II: Develop preliminary vehicle design concepts, a demonstrator system, and demonstration plans.

- FATE II: Develop, build and flight-test a demonstrator vehicle to achieve program goals.

FATE I, Phase I was used as a jump-start for the Uninhabited Combat Air Vehicle Advanced Technology Demonstration (UCAV ATD), X-45 that effectively replaced the FATE program, which studied the major benefits of tailless aircraft, design. In the past, tailless aircraft directional control has been provided by spoilers or drag rudders. This was done to de-couple the control system as much as possible. Unfortunately, spoilers and drag rudders have high attendant actuator requirements (a result of large hinge moments) and provide inadequate control power at high AoA.

X-36 model in N-212, Model Development & Advanced Composites at NASA. NASA

'With quantum advances in throughput capabilities of digital processors, it is now possible to take advantage of advanced integrated/adaptive flight control techniques that make a decoupled control effector a requirement. As a result, more efficient aerodynamic controls, like the all-moving wing tip or spoiler-slot-deflector, can now be used for tailless aircraft lateral-directional control. Integration of these effectors reduces control suite weight fraction 5%, reduces hydraulic power requirements 45% (because hinge moments are much less than those of conventional surfaces), and vastly improves high AoA flying qualities. All of these factors contribute to improved agility.

Advanced flight control technologies that enable these unconventional effectors also reduce FCS complexity and cost and will reduce loss-of-control related accidents and mission-critical vulnerability.'

Benefits of the various tailless technologies include

- Reduced drag (compared to a tailed airplane), reduced weight (compared to a 1995 SOA tail-less aircraft).

- Improved high-AoA agility and flying qualities.

- Reduced actuator redundancy requirements.

- Reduced number of Operational Flight Program (OFP) design cycles.

- Reduced control-related accidents and mission-critical vulnerability.

The last three improvements are attributable to the integrated/adaptive controls technologies rather than the innovative control effectors. These improvements would be available to any configuration employing this type of flight control system, not just tailless aircraft. Finally, the enabler for all of these technologies is the new high-throughput processor now available for the flight control computer.

Drag Reduction Potential of Tailless Designs

Minimum drag data for two configurations employing vertical tails shows that the vertical tail accounts for 5% to 10% of the total airplane minimum drag at a cruise Mach number of 0.9. Configuration features like area distribution and interference affects results in variation of the tail contribution. Nevertheless, 5% CDmin is still significant.

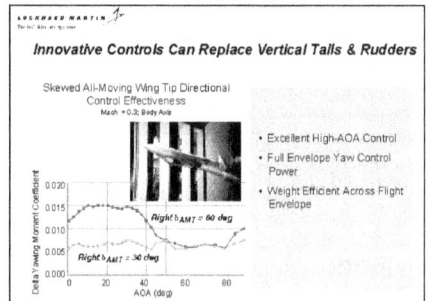

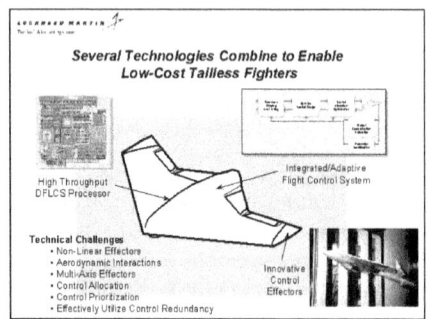

Top and above: These diagrams show Lockheed Martins studies into combining MATV and innovative controls to provide future tailless aircraft with complete envelope control. Both Lockheed Martin

The only one of the two X-36 vehicles to fly is now displayed in the Research and Development Gallery at the National Museum of the USAF at Wright Patterson AFB, Ohio. USAFM Below: Seen at Dryden during its test program, the X-36 program has contributed to the pathway leading to the Uninhabited Combat Air Vehicles demonstration programs conducted in the early 21st Century. NASA

Data from low-speed wind tunnel tests conducted during the Innovative Control Effectors (ICE) program show that the all-moving wing tip provides substantial yawing moments through 90-degrees AoA. The magnitude of the yaw power available is sufficient to provide Level 1 flying qualities to this vehicle. The high AoA directional control power available is superior to that available from vertical tail/rudder controls, which greatly improves agility levels. Together with multi-axis thrust vectoring, innovative controls can provide tailless aircraft with full envelope control, including unparalleled high AoA agility.

All-Moving Wing Tips and Spoiler-Slot-Deflectors Are Weight-Efficient Tailless Controls

An efficiency parameter was computed by dividing the control power available (DCn) by the weight of the effector and its actuator. The clamshell, typically used by previous tailless aircraft, has good weight efficiency at low dynamic pressure conditions. However, the high hinge moments associated with this control contribute to very poor high-speed efficiency. Furthermore, at high AoA, flow separation causes adverse roll-yaw characteristics that limit the usefulness of this surface during roll co-ordination. Both the all-moving wing tip and the spoiler-slot-deflector exhibit much smaller high-speed hinge moments, and are more efficient than the clamshell. A

Top: The first X-45A UCAV Demonstrator during its 6th flight on 19 December 2002: Above: The second X-45A vehicle during its maiden flight in November 2002. Both NASA

rudder has excellent weight efficiency throughout the majority of the AoA envelope, but suffers at high AoA as it loses effectiveness. At low speeds (low dynamic pressures), TV is the most efficient of any of the effectors. However, thrust vectoring control effectiveness falls off rapidly at high dynamic pressures, and its efficiency suffers. The all-moving wing tip provides good weight efficiency in all flight conditions (although not the best

The Northrop Grumman X-47A UCAV Demonstrator seen at its roll-out (top) was a small scale 'Kite' like design, which led directly to the larger X-47B, seen (above) during its second flight in 2011. Both Northrop Grumman

at any given one) and, therefore, is a good choice for tailless aircraft control. The spoiler-slot-deflector ranks second in this regard. Note that weight efficiency is as good as that of the F-16 rudder in the high-speed low-AoA condition.

Tailless Aircraft Risks/Penalties Compared with Those of Tailed Aircraft

There are also penalties and risks to be addressed when designing tailless aircraft when compared to conventional tailed aircraft. Penalties of choosing a tailless configuration include:

- Increased structural weight - A vertical tail and rudder are still the most weight efficient directional control and stabilisation device for most of the flight envelope.
- Increased hydraulic power requirements - Primarily this increase is caused by increased actuator rate requirements of the innovative effectors.
- Increased FCS complexity. A tailless design incorporating innovative controls drives the configuration to include the integrated/adaptive flight control algorithms to mitigate the complexity involved with using traditional control design philosophies.

Integration of innovative controls may compromise wing camber design on some configurations. This depends on planform and mission, and applies to wings having no leading-edge flaps. Note that the spoiler-slot-deflector controls do not carry this penalty."

The first of two Boeing X-45 UCAV (Uninhabited Combat Air Vehicle) demonstrators' was rolled-out at St Louis, Missouri in September 2000. The X-45 can trace its lineage back to the X-36, with much of the latter technology being incorporated into the X-45.

The goal of the joint DARPA/USAF UCAV ATD (Advanced Technology Demonstrator) program was to demonstrate the technical feasibility for an UCAV system to effectively and affordably conduct suppression of enemy air defences and strike missions.

The X-45C was an evolution of the X-45B, which was itself a planned larger variant of the X-45A aimed at the J-UCAS (Joint Uninhabited Combat Air System) program, which was subsequently cancelled. Boeing

The X-45A system included a stealthy, tailless 27-ft long, 8,000-lb (empty) vehicle with a 34-ft wing span. The vehicle had a re-configurable mission control system with robust satellite-relay and line-of-sight communications links for distributed control in all air combat situations; and a supportability approach that included long-term, compact storage, periodic systems testing and re-assembly for flight in just over an hour. It was powered by a Honeywell F124 turbofan engine, which is apparently not visible from the frontal aspect. The engine was fitted with a low observable thrust-vectoring nozzle, which was fully integrated with the aircraft's flight control system, allowing thrust vectoring to be used in place of vertical tails, drawing on experience gained during the X-36 program.

Boeing and Northrop Grumman also entered the competition to build an UCAV demonstrator for the USN with both companies receiving 15-month contracts for the first phase of the UCAV-N program, which would eventually lead to the Northrop Grumman X-47B UCAV-N

NASA Dryden Flight Research Centre is still involved in tailless flight research flying the large-scale X-48B Blended-Wing-Body research aircraft, which has no vertical tail, but does have very large winglets and engines mounted on top of the rear fuselage. NASA

Demonstrator, which conducted its maiden flight on 4 February 2011.

As well as the X-45 and UCAV-N programs, several other UCAV programs have emerged, with some falling by the wayside and others leading to further research program. Lockheed Martin received a six-month USN contract to define a family of UCAV's which could be launched from ships and submarines to attack high-value fixed targets or SEAD within a range of 1,100-km (600-nm). Under the six month USN contract, Lockheed Martin was defining three notional UCAV UNSA concepts. The three included STOVL and Vertical-Attitude Take-off and Landing (VATOL) which

would be suitable for deployment for surface vessel launch and recovery. Most of the designs studied incorporated either full or quasi-tailless configurations.

Not long after the X-45 rollout, the French manufacturer Dassault shocked its competitors by revealing that it had flight-tested a sub-scale, tailless UCAV demonstrator during July 2000. Dassault revealed that the vehicle was controlled using three flaperons on each wing. Several programs are now underway in Europe including the French AVE.

Retired following its RESTORE flight test phase, the only one of the X-36 flight Vehicles to fly has been inducted into the National Museum of the USAF at Wright Patterson AFB, Ohio having been delivered in April 2003. Although retired, the X-36 legacy lives on in the plethora of tailless aircraft studies being conducted in this early part of the 21st Century.

Weights

TOGW....................1,245 lb
O.W.E.....................1,083 lb
Usable Fuel.............162 lb
Thrust Class..............700 lb
Density.................28.3 lb/ft^3

Performance

Mach Number.................≤0.6
G_{Limit}...............................5 g's
q_{Limit}...........................200 psf
Landing Gear...............14 fps
$V_{Approach}$..................112 KEAS
Max AOA.......................~ 35°

Materials

Skin - Carbon Epoxy and Aluminum
Bones - Machined Aluminum
Assembly - Mechanical Attachment
Nozzle - Cast Chem Mill Titanium

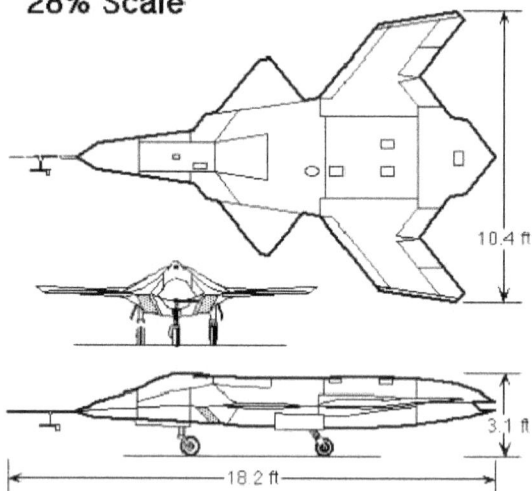

28% Scale

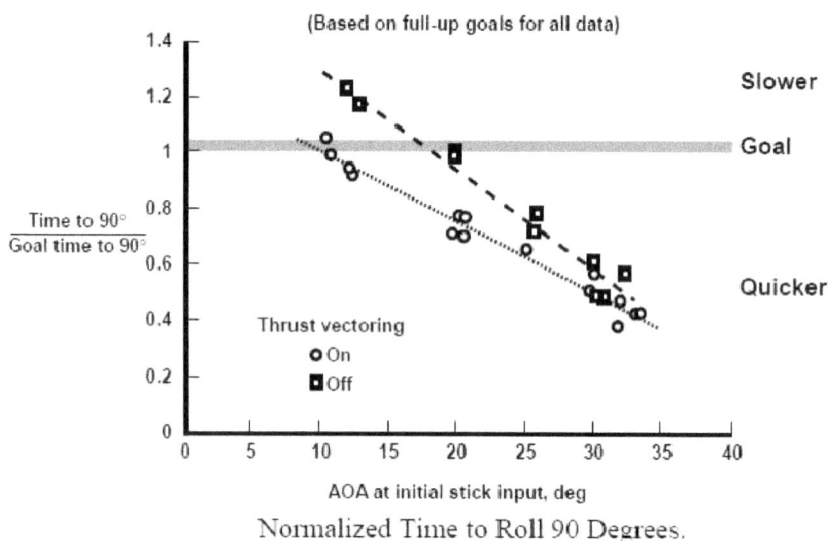

Normalized Time to Roll 90 Degrees.

44

SPECIFICATION

Boeing/NASA X-36

Type: Uninhabited sub-scale, tailless fighter technology demonstrator.
Manufacturer: McDonnell Douglas Corporation (now Boeing).
Materials: Skin - carbon epoxy and aluminium; Bones - machined aluminium; Assembly - mechanical attachment; Nozzle - cast chem mill titanium.
Power plant: A single William's International F112 turbofan rated at 3.1 kN (700-lb).
Density: 28.3-lb/ft3.
Dimensions: Wing span 3.6 m (11 ft); length of 6.3 m (19 ft); height 1 m (3 ft).
Weights: Empty 492-kg (1,083-lb) and maximum take-off 590 kg (1,298-lb).
Fuel load: 162-lb.
Performance: Maximum speed for test program, 160-kt (300-km/h); maximum Mach number = Mach 0.6; maximum attained speed; 234-mph.
Ceiling: Maximum attained ceiling; 20,200-ft - 20,500-ft
G-Limit: 5-g.
Q-Limit: 200-psf.
Landing gear: 14-fps.
V Approach: 112 KEAS
Maximum AoA: 35-degrees design (40-degrees was achieved during the flight test program).
Crew: Uninhabited

Glossary

AAW	Active Aero elastic Wing
ACTIVE	Active Control Technology for Integrated Vehicles
AFB	Air Force Base
AoA	Angle Of Attack
ATA	Advanced Tactical Aircraft
ATD	Advanced Technology Demonstrator
ATF	Advanced Tactical Fighter
BAe	British Aerospace
DARPA	Defence Advanced Research Projects Agency
DFRC	Dryden Flight Research Centre
FATE	Future Aircraft Technology Enhancement
FBW	Fly-By-Wire
FCS	Flight Control System
FOAS	Future Offensive Air System
FWV	Fixed Wing Vehicle
HiMAT	Highly Manoeuvrable Aircraft Technology
HOTAS	Hands On Throttle and Stick
HUD	Heads Up Display
ICE	Innovative Control Effectors
JSF	Joint Strike Fighter
JSPO	Joint Strike Fighter Program Office
J-UCAS	Joint Uninhabited Combat Air System
KEAS	Knots Equivalent Air Speed
Kt or Kts	Knots
LCA	Light Combat Aircraft
MATV	Multi-Axis Thrust Vectoring
MBB	Messerchmitt-Bolkow-Blohm
MCA	Medium Combat Aircraft
MDC	McDonnell Douglas Corporation
NASA	National Aeronautics and Space Administration
NAVAIR	Naval Air Systems Command
NG	Northrop Grumman
OFP	Operational Flight Program
PAV	Prototype Air Vehicle
PID	Parameter Identification
RESTORE	Re-configurable Systems for Tailless Fighter Aircraft
RTSM	Real Time Stability Margin
SEAD	Suppression of Enemy Air Defence
STOVL	Short Take-Off and Vertical Landing
TV	Thrust Vector
UCAV	Uninhabited Combat Air Vehicle
UCAV-N	Uninhabited Combat Air Vehicle-Naval
UNSA	Uninhabited Naval Strike Aircraft
USAF	United States Air Force
USN	Unites States Navy
VATOL	Vertical-Attitude Take-off and Landing
VECTOR	Vectoring Extremely short take-off and landing Control and Tailless Operation Research

Centurion Publishing 2013

$\mathcal{CP}$

www.ingramcontent.com/pod-product-compliance
Lightning Source LLC
LaVergne TN
LVHW052151080426
835511LV00009B/1798